The Quiet.

THE QUIET.

POEMS. BY

ANNE-MARIE TURZA.

ANANSI

This edition published in 2014 by

House of Anansi Press Inc.,
110 Spadina Ave., Suite 801
Toronto, ON,
M5V 2K4
Tel. 416-363-4343
Fax 416-363-1017
**www.
houseofanansi.com**

Distributed in Canada by

*HarperCollins
Canada Ltd.*
1995 Markham Rd.,
Scarborough, ON, M1B 5M8
Toll free tel.
1-800-387-0117

Distributed in
the United States by

*Publishers
Group West*
1700 Fourth St.,
Berkeley, CA 94710
Toll free tel.
1-800-788-3123

House of Anansi Press is committed to protecting our natural environment. As part of our efforts, the interior of this book is printed on paper made from second-growth forests and is acid-free.

18 17 16 15 14   1 2 3 4 5

*Library and Archives Canada
Cataloguing in Publication*
Turza, Anne-Marie, 1976 –,
author
The quiet / Anne-Marie Turza.

Issued in print and electronic formats.
ISBN 978-1-77089-808-0 (bound)
—ISBN 978-1-77089-443-3 (pbk.)
—ISBN 978-1-77089-444-0 (pdf)
I. Title.
PS8639.U79Q85 2014
C811'.6
C2013-907038-9   C2013-907039-7

*Library of Congress Control
Number:*
2013918888

Cover design: Brian Morgan
Text design and typesetting:
Brian Morgan

We acknowledge for their financial support of our publishing program the Canada Council for the Arts, the Ontario Arts Council, and the Government of Canada through the Canada Book Fund.

Printed and bound in Canada

I drowned long ago. I drowned in that country.
— *Melanie Siebert*

That's when I married the cat of water.
My face pressed to the space where space had only just
ended, Space of space, empty, ô air.
— *Erín Moure*

Contents.

THE QUIET

NOT MINE, NOT ANYONE'S

THE QUIET

THE QUIET

i:i

—And its sound?
—As in the toothed whale. There is a buried hearing organ.

—And its sound?
—It enters the immersed body firstmost through the throat.

i:ii

You could say: slender, long-legged. Dark or with length-wise dark-and-light stripes. Covered with long hair. Upper row of large eyes. But that is the Thin-Legged Wolf Spider. Not its quiet. Its quiet isn't known to anyone but the spider.

i:iii

Within every city are unseen cities, intangible walls and alleys: a voice, one afternoon on the radio, addressed its audience. Rats too are historiographers, said the voice, the voice of a rat specialist. Come hydraulic hammers and hoe rams, come rubble. Rats thread the empty plots between ghost buildings, following old paths to their nests as if the walls still stand. In this city of brick and limestone where you and I are sleeping. Every night, traversing pathways that seem no longer to exist.

The quiet is not unlike the ink sketches found in Satie's room soon after his death, a room no one else had entered in twenty-seven years. In the room: love letters; seven velvet suits; many umbrellas, an unspecified number, never used; musical scores. "It seems to me that I am cursed." Satie said this, in a letter to a friend. Also: "I'm free, free as air, as water, as the wild sheep." The sketches, of medieval buildings, drawn on small cards of stiff paper. Sometimes he put ads in the local dailies: "For sale, castle of lead."

The tardigrade or water bear. Without fur and microscopic. It lumbers slowly in the ambit of a centimeter. Mouth circular and open, curiously like a christmas orange, peeled, and flowering into segments.

Transparent. Curved minutely.
How like claws its claws are.

One says: it was smaller then. And one: it was larger, so large, its sound was elsewhere. And one: as in measurements. Counting the charged particles. One says: it's close and scalpiform. And one: it slips from everything, in all directions.

i:vii

A man is sewing button holes into the wings of moths.
The wings tear, and the man keeps sewing. It is long ago.
The world still has an end. The man carries the moths
there. Gently. They begin their long falling.

NOT MINE,
NOT ANYONE'S

HOUSEHOLDS

"... of unknown origin,
perhaps connected to the root of hide *(v.)."*
—house, *the Etymology Dictionary*

Have you a house like mine, with doors to other houses?
One cupboard, whenever it's cracked, smells damply of threes:
a roadside cross, snowfall, a bell of glass

ringing darkly in a house from another century.
A boy lives there, with his stranger's life.
As for mine: it too, ringing darkly.

The job of a house is to have a roof.
And the job of a life? It might be anything,
made of wood or drift or warning.

"With his familiar face but terrible eyes, he was coming along,
stumbling over the hummocks . . ."
— *Tolstoy,* Anna Karenina

To the wetlands, past the gaunt trunks of spruce and
stands of willow girding the sinkhole lakes, through a
forest of yellow birch Levin has come, slinging his shotgun.
Purple-red dogwoods and a green creek, his dog riffing
the water with her tongue. Here, he hunkers down. This
morning,

the blown-glass light. Diaphanous and fragile, a curio,
lying on the bedroom floor. What else could be bodied,
and so thin: that light: almost nothing inside its shell. In
such light, it seems wrong to think of objects without first
touching them. Curved and cool, the pewter handle of a
boot brush. Or a loose thread from the silk scarf floating on
a hook behind the door. Light so spare it's almost darkness.
That light filled the room with scantness, lessening the oak
rocker to a rack of bone.

Because it is the season of sudden rain it begins now to
rain as if every raindrop must fall at once: the sky is a cold
body of bolting water; Levin's dog, somewhere ahead: her
worried yammer. The rain's blether grows louder, a gallop
of hard consonants Levin feels he could understand, were
it slower—

In the sea are lobsters, long in body as two tall men,
    alive one hundred years. And a church bell meant for an island,

    never steeple-rung, sunk with the *Genevieve* and all hands.
No one asks what I believe. And I would not say very loudly:

I believe in ice, in ice only. It's true,
    there is no kind of original earthworm in this country,

    all were ice-killed. The old glaciers,
million-ton frontal planes culling millennial topsoil.

Do twelve-foot lobsters seem not as improbable as gods?
    Feelers in lengthy syncopation, eyes

    deep occupied manholes.
Here one can live at any dark system's edge—

underwater canyons, sewers, storms, stars—
    know little about, and die of it, being old.

Terminal winter, our skulls painted with coal dust.
    A bell blessed in the ship's punched hull, plunging down.

HERE, BOY

"You must look for mushrooms and it follows that you may not find them," says Sergej Timofeevich Aksakov, in his *Remarks and Observations of a Mushroom Hunter*. We throw rounds of sausage up into the branches, not high enough: in a shower of sparse ordinary needles the colour of ripe apricots, something must have happened, we tell each other, what, what! How did the dog get up into the pine tree? Through the needles, the sere-green bursts, in the high branches, we can see its ruff like a froth of common milk. It's daylight. We're in the pine grove, hunting yellow chanterelles. The dog begins to carol.

ANIMALCULES

—Term dating from the
first sighting of unicellular organisms
in the 17th century.

I tend the little animals
on one eyelash.

It's no different than hopscotch
to blink, not harming them.

Like clouds, they amass
subaltern histories.

"Que sais-je?" says Montaigne
to the little animals.

Are they hurt by wind.
What else is likely.

THE GLASS CASE

The girl when very young was sealed in a glass case, lowered with ropes into the river. With her, in the case: a dry branch and sizable dust, else, nothing; still, she reached a mature age there. The glass case froze in ice beneath a bridge. I looked down through ice a clouded untold distance, and saw her legs, thin and darkened. I did not see the rest of her. The ones who lowered her in the water sang: Did you eat up the branch? Did you eat up the dust? Little Mary, Little Mary.

AFTER THE BEDTIME STORY

Like a spill of dark water over the sill of the window the boy has left open to let in the smell of rain, the black rabbits stream. They surge across the floorboards, bristling, rattling their claws. Where the floor dips, they gather. Breathing in the far corner of the room. There they crouch, wild in their fur. Wheeling eyes. The boy peers from his bed. "Again," he tells them. These are his rabbits. They lurch up on their hind legs.

ANTHEM FOR A SMALL COUNTRY

In my country we admire the ambitious dust: long into the night,
for endless hours, it practices such gentleness on the window's sill.

Our country's flower is the rose in the curved bed of the fingernail.
In the cloud's menagerie, our animal is the solitary wisp.

As for religion, we peer into drains and the old burrows
of earthworms, looking for our shrinking god.

Our territory often dwindles to a smooth slip
of a pillow, a fleece blanket and the bed's four posts.

What we lack in fellow citizens, we address by mumbling
to ourselves. And to the white cat, and the calico.

From the industry of sleep, exporting
small, domestic sounds.

NOT MINE, NOT ANYONE'S,

the god that is leaving,
leaving snow to be snow
of what kinds /of its kinds.

Snow of lit vestibules.
Snow shadowed with algebra.
Snow of many crystalline ears.

And the others, the other snows, falling.

Small now, smaller even than that—

do you think so too?—
we will need to be lost

in the drifts
in the drifts

in the back garden.

[AND THEN . . .]

And then we were unborn, three girls about to meet our mother for the first time. We donned our shindig ties and collars, we blacked our sheepskin slippers, we crowded the rope ladder. The forward weather was decades large. Our mother, in a silent film. A nurse arrived with dime store bags of ice, two small bags of clear plastic. Goldfish swam in black and white among the ice cubes. The glare above the bed made the fish invisible. She will donate her retinas, said the nurse's mouth in cursive letters. She placed the bags of ice, first one, and then the other, on our mother's closed eyes.

A year passed, and another year, and I was old. I had a
visitor, a woman who knelt on my porch, sewing clothes for
a collection of dolls she believed I kept concealed beneath
the chesterfield, in the wardrobe, somewhere close to us
in my unlit rooms.

I told her I had no dolls. But her percussive fingers and
the needle flashing in the rich fabrics never slowed. "For
the doll with the dancing shoes," she said, shaking out a
miniature overskirt printed with velvet bulls. And a bour-
bon cloak of ripped silk: "For the doll with one gold tooth."

It's true, I admired her intricate knots, a hand-dyed shirt-
waist with a row of crystal buttons glowing like a line of
clear glass eyes: even now, I hear her thimble on my door,
its glottal toc toc toc. My neighbours have begun to say
they live near the house of dolls. It might well be so. Last
night at my insistence, a doll widowed by a Russian prince,
a doll I'm sure is somewhere, acquired a long veil of black
lace stitched on my porch while I looked on.

Who can say yes or no in these months of little sleep.
I'm told that moths aren't drawn to the bulb, but to the
darkness just beyond it, the darkness light intensifies. This
explains their circling.

THE QUIET

We lived in that quiet, above megrims in second storey windows, painted our mouths with ketchup, our eyelids with sweet relish, wore singlets made from the dyed hair of miniature horses. Evenings, we lit candles. Chanted in Latin. *Adsum, adsum, a capite ad calcem.* Mostly we didn't know what we were saying. We lived there for years, shared our beds with the mouths of beetles. In that quiet, tender with attention, our faces swollen, the stung backs of our knees, our bitten heels.

ii:ii

—And its sound?
—A nerve ran through it, like the long nerve in the eyetooth
   of a cat.
—Its sound was pointed?
—In the ear's direction. Yes.

ii:iii

Ten miles above the house, the sky thins to nothing.

Ten miles above the house—

The quiet is not unlike the pitches thrown by Satchel Paige in the late 1920s for the Birmingham Black Barons. He threw the ball as far from the bat and as close to the plate as possible, said Casey Stengel, who was called the Old Perfessor. Hesitation Pitch. Be Ball. Four-Day Creeper. Bat Dodger. The Barber. Nothin' Ball.

ii:v

The woman's feet, raised with pillows. A cork pinned with a long needle to the end of every toe. The skeletons are yellow and clean. They circle the bed. En l'air, leg bones in unison. Their fingers are much longer, the woman thinks, now that the palms are gone.

It is said the potato bug cries like a child. This is untrue.
Neither does it eat the potato in any part. It is not from
Jerusalem. Still, it is called the Jerusalem cricket.

Elsewhere, stone cricket.
Niña de la tierra.
Awake at night and solitary.
Who lives a single year, mostly underground.

ii:vii

A man on the back of a snow bear in a narrow alley of
tenements, the mudbrick tower houses of the walled city.
People lean through the high windows, looking down.
Some of them are pointing. The man, burred on the bear's
thick neck, his arms straked in its fur. He might be hurt, or
sleeping. He might be overcome in the trial of hanging on.
No one can tell. To be just, Simone Weil said, it is necessary
to be naked and dead. *There is infinite hope, but not for us.*

45

OTHER BUZZING PASSAGE

Have you never met, in passing, a stranger who addressed you knowingly? "You can't sleep well, in your language," a woman once told me, pipe smoke seeping from the bowl of her vowels. I was reading a book with a soft cloth cover, a monograph on the water beetle, waiting for a train in the glass-domed station, the pages stippled with dust. The woman pointed to a table where a man sat eating almonds from a green bowl. "In my language I can put that table anywhere." Pardon me?, I said. Already, the table, drifting upwards; tendrils of the man's hair, on end; the smooth soles of his shoes, eighth notes rising overhead. A rain of almonds from the high dome where birdshapes turn millwheel in the gathered clangour of the trains. To sleep well, not in this language.

ROCK PAPER SCISSORS AUTOBIOGRAPHY

Scissors, scissors: I too love molecules. To separate one from another, in fact, so they are rare and lonely.

Rock blunts scissors: a rattling, crooked and purple, cartwheels upward, whistling with light. I am blind, I do not yet know it.

Scissors cut paper: sudden, I come upon the door to a little room where a woman with a skin hat, never met, has been for mute years, living.

Paper, paper: I would like to censor my reflection. It doesn't know me.

Paper covers rock: a cross-hatched hollow, sometimes with a mouse inside. It was her eye. Her hair in granite lines. She is dead, I will draw her body.

Rock, rock: whereas, let it be resolved. I called through a glass door, the house dogs leapt up barking.

LAST HOUR

He swam without air elderly and east in the warrens of
his veins his lungs two ton magnets in the pull of banished
animals. Diplomystus brevissimus fish splay of Eocene
bones prickling in his temporal lobe. Other things were
there tunnelling east southeast away from him. He swam
in a white nightshirt. He swam with his eyes shut. He had
once pencilled a question mark in the corner of an envelope
next to a bright stamp: it was printed with some kind of
blue and gold flower.

HAUNT

"Probably from O.N. heimta bring home."
—the Etymology Dictionary

There was a sky. It issued types of certain rain.
Or vacancy. Or a grim saluting front. We saw by that.

We were temporal and various in drywall rooms.
Sloe hedges on a corner lot. The berries sized like nailheads:

those were ours. Beneath the beds, shoes in doublets
of different temperaments. Our persons,

carried about with us from room to room, passing hourlike
in the hall, might speak or blink or do nothing outward.
   We became

the specifics, i.e., an amalgam of accidents. This year,
that year, iced cakes, singular rustlings.

What else? We were mortal. In case of gods
we planned to gather as we could, in the gravel drive.

LEVIN AS A CHILD

"So he lived, not knowing and not seeing any possibility of knowing
what he was and why he lived in the world . . ."
—Tolstoy, Anna Karenina

One of those candle-eyed children—you know them by the
steep staircase they seem always to be climbing, as if it's
autumn, a sheer rain is sleeving, and confined in a house of
oak, they're hoping to reach the eaves, a small window on a
wooden hinge that might be swinging open there—his head
bare, the damp curl on his forehead a sign of fever. This is
the world: a gray wolfhound down in the yard, her belly in
the mud, muzzle tipped with dripping fur.

DEAR GOD
—AND WHEN I SAY GOD, I MEAN THE GOD

who made the snail, curled in a perfect house,
shitting on its own head; I mean the god

of untrue colours, the chartreuse and teal
god; I mean god of the conditional

tense, in the dark on the sixth day, who said
If there had been light: and there had been light.

I mean that god. I mean: Dear thick-kneed god,
Dear god who wears shoes big, who shambles—

PINCHER CREEK

Our mother in Woolworth's, thin—
I assure you—as a rawboned child, pulling black blouses
from the children's racks, her children asking
how long until he's bones?, reckoning
the months a body in the ground
might last. The grassland plot, frozen.
To sink a pick-mattock in winter, set a fire.

Windthrow smouldering in the mound.

LEVIN IN LOVE

"And what he saw then, he never saw again."
—*Tolstoy*, Anna Karenina

Halfway through that story of gilt sofas and suicide by train—halfway, almost exactly—Levin, in love, cannot button his coat. You understand: this is not the story Tolstoy told, or at least, not what Tolstoy told us. The difference: Levin is here, with us, his fingers slipping among the pewter buttons, fastening them crookedly: we see the gaps, those lapses in the thick fabric of the greatcoat, exposing his shirtfront beneath which we can hear, almost, the trammelling heart: his fingers slip, he cannot, cannot button his coat. We must make his hands clumsy, we must delay him. Soon enough, he'll go half-dressed into the street, he'll see "the greyish-blue pigeons . . . and the little loaves of bread, sprinkled with flour, that some invisible hand had put outside the baker's shop." Somehow we must keep him here with us. Levin new in love. Soon enough, he'll see what moves him most. A loaf of bread, a pigeon, fluttering its wings in the commonplace, the snow glittering, extraordinary. What he'll never see again.

BARREN

Not in the branches of the pitch pine, waxing its wood cones.
Neither in the grass's rhizomes thickening the ground.

Nowhere in the real will I divine you.
Not in the shards of stones. Not in the shade of stones.

Neither in the blue tint of the stones' shade.
Noplace in the air. Your eye. Tell me: what's caught

your eye? Not the fern, now uncurling, sporing
its split leaves. Where then is your attention held?

I'm barren and I am your mother. Discarnate child,

yours is the stark eye that can't be born.
The naughting eye: and nothing after.

OTHER BUZZING PASSAGE

*"My team members and I don't know what it is. We've tried to find
out, but each time something forces us to turn back: a spike in carbon
monoxide, a breathing-mask failure, a choking blast of ammonia. Now
I'm trying again. But the passage is narrowing."*
—speleologist Penelope Boston

Diasporic seeds, hurricane-blown perhaps
into the salt water hills, the ocean's
flooding drift: cream yellow nickernut
and gray; the sea purse; sea heart; and the true
sea bean. *That* there *are*: submarine rivers;
benthic lakes; most immense water-fall, ever
crashing // over a bluff made of water

some how, within the ocean. There is fire
too, from volcanoes, many plumed thousands
on the sea floor; ice spires and blind cracklings;
orchestral clocks of sponge; cases of stairs
out of pressed gases; shock-green animals
we've hardly seen, their vestments copious,
billowing in the deep kilometers.

Further from the earth, every year, by four
centimeters. How far is that. Just so:
O, O, o, o, the moon is more distant.
Like a mote it shall be, in however
many biblical increments. The tides
will stop! Then, the journals of a painter
who lived earlier in eons, when

the sea, a dark greenish blue like a fig,
beat on the shore: well, if we were alive
still, wouldn't it mean something. Meanwhile
I'm yet myself, wanting to ask about
Cueva de Villa Luz, the sulfur cave,
acid drip dripping in the sure black
at the back of the fissure too narrow

to get to. Whatever is buzzing.

THE QUIET

The quiet is not unlike that long crescent-shaped lake of freshwater seals, that body of water at times blue, at times blue-green, called the North Sea in Chinese texts of the third century, near the city of Irkutsk in Siberia, lake Baikal—a lake so deep a boulder, dropped centermost, would sink the length of the CN tower once twice three times, and would still not reach its ground—there in the depths, the golomyanka, a transparent oil fish that lays no eggs, gives birth to its young, live. Above, on the surface, the fishermen sing the old chant to the wind, using its name: Hey, *barguzin*, drive the waves harder, we haven't far to go.

iii:ii

Beetles in the plaster walls. Beetles with ears beneath their wings.

iii:iii

How many cells are needed
to feel solitary. Or

x is greater than.

iii:iv

At the front of a school bus, a burned girl in a protective suit. Like a keeper of bees. The tight shine of her face. Furrowed, draped in netting.

iii:v

Now the northern wooden roads, made of logs, pounded on their ends into the permafrost, locked in the ground and slowly sinking.

New logs pounded in above the sunken logs, strata of wooden roads in the locked ground, sinking.

iii:vi

Has it a bright carapace, antennae of dissolving bone?

iii:vii

The midwife harnessed ten white housecats to her bobsled. The streets jittered with the high-pitched tin of bells the size of molars.

In the air the cold slid open like tiers of miniature windows.

.

Notes.

THE QUIET I:II: "...slender, long-legged. Dark or with lengthwise dark-and-light stripes. Covered with long hair. Upper row of large eyes." *National Audubon Society Field Guide to North American Insects and Spiders.*

THE QUIET I:IV: quotations from Erik Satie's letters are taken from Robert Orledge's *Satie the Composer.* "I'm free, free as air..." translated by Michael Bullock.

THE QUIET II:VII: quotation from Simone Weil as rendered in a translation of *Gravity and Grace* by Emma Crawford and Mario von der Ruhr. "There is infinite hope, but not for us." An epigram of Kafka's.

HERE, BOY: quotation from Sergej Timofeevich Aksakov's *Remarks and Observations of a Mushroom Hunter*, translated by Valentina Pavlovna Wasson.

ANIMALCULES: "Que sais-je?" What do I know? Michel de Montaigne.

OTHER BUZZING PASSAGE is the name of a geographical feature in Cueva de Villa Luz, a sulphur cave in Tabasco, Mexico. "The sea, a dark greenish blue like a fig," is a line from the journals of Eugène Delacroix.

THE QUIET III:I: The fisherman's song to the wind appeared in Ed Struzik's article "Passage to Baikal," *Equinox* Magazine, May/June 1991.

QUOTATIONS FROM *Anna Karenina* were selected from a translation by David Magarshack.

77

Acknowledgements.

TO Sara Peters, who edited this book. I'm very grateful for her skillful attention and care.

TO Brian Morgan, who designed the cover and interior.

TO the House of Anansi Press. In particular, I'd like to thank Sarah MacLachlan, Kelly Joseph, Laura Repas, Meredith Dees, and Matt Williams.

TO Jared Bland, who read this manuscript with generosity and accepted it for publication.

TO Lorna Crozier, who has taught me a great deal with the perfect balance of rigour and humour.

TO Tim Lilburn, Martin Adams, Nicholas Bradley, and the Creative Writing Department at the University of Victoria.

TO the people of the Coast Salish Nation. The greater part of this book was written on Coast Salish land.

TO the Anishinabe peoples. This book was completed in the territory of the Algonquin Nation.

TO the translators of the works that have enriched this project.

TO the Canada Council for the Arts.

TO *Arc Poetry Magazine*, *The Antigonish Review*, *The Malahat Review*, *Grain Magazine*, *The New Quarterly*, *Prism International*, *Prairie Fire*, Tightrope Books, and Kore Press, Open Space, and the Writers' Trust of Canada for previous appearances of poems.

TO Dave Bennett, who featured lines from several of these poems in the *garagenoper "Auf der Suche Nach der Nordwestpassage."*

TO Martin Silver, who featured lines from the poems in several songs.

TO Patrick Corbeil, James Bennett, Andrea Smith, Anne Hutchison, John Pollard, and Sabrina Schroeder, who introduced me to animals, concepts, or figures appearing here.

TO Melanie Siebert, Ali Blythe, Sadiqa de Meijir, and Garth Martens, who read multiple versions of this manuscript and provided such generous feedback and support. Thank you, my dear friends.

THIS BOOK IS FOR John Howard Bennett and Thomas Kenneth Richard Bourns, my fathers. I wish they could have met.

79

ANNE-MARIE TURZA's work has appeared in *Arc Poetry Magazine*, *The Malahat Review*, and the anthology *The Best Canadian Poetry in English 2010*, among others. Her home is Victoria, British Columbia.